CHANGE
Rewire Your Mind

How to Get Unstuck, Stop Beating Yourself Up, Stop Self Sabotage, and Stop Living in the Past Without Drugs, Antidepressants or Years in Therapy.

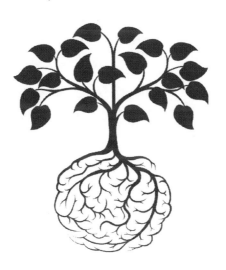

By Christy Mattoon

Christy Mattoon and Mind Rewire LLC
6834 University Blvd
Suite 160
Centennial Co. 80122

Limits of Liability and Disclaimer

The author and publisher shall not be liable for your misuse of this content, or material. This book is strictly for informational and educational purposes only.

Copyright Use and Public Information

Unless noted images have been used with permission from owner and are keeping with public information laws. Please contact Author for questions about copyrights or the use of public information.

General Information

With a clear subconscious : Thinking positive thoughts will lead to positive action. Use at your own discretion.

ISBN 13: 978-1980264415

DISCLAIMER

The author and publisher of this training program and the accompanying materials have used their best efforts in preparing this training program. The author and publisher make no representation or warranties regarding with respect to accuracy, application. Fitness, or completeness of the contents of this book. Therefore if you wish to apply ideas contained in this training program, you take full responsibility for your actions.

EVERY EFFORT HAS BEEN MADE TO ACCURATELY REPRESENT THIS PRODUCT AND ITS POTENTIAL. EVEN AS THIS INDUSTRY IS RAPIDLY CHANGING AND HEALING SPONTANEOUSLY IS ON THE RISE- THERE IS NO GUARANTEE THAT YOU WILL SEE A SPONTANEOUS OR MIRACULOUS HEALING IN REGARDS TO THIS PRODUCT.

ANY CLAIMS MADE OF MIRACULOUS CHANGES OR SPONTANEOUS HEALINGS CAN BE VERIFIED UPON REQUEST. YOUR LEVEL OF SUCCESS IN OBTAINING THE RESULTS CLAIMED IN THIS BOOK OR IN OUR MATERIALS DEPENDS ON THE TIME AND EFFORT YOU DEVOTE TO YOUR OWN EFFORT AND PROGRESS. I CAN NOT GUARANTEE YOUR SUCCESS AND AM NOT RESPONSIBLE FOR YOUR ACTIONS AS FACTORS DIFFER ACCORDING TO INDIVIDUALS.

The author and publisher shall in no event be held liable to any party for any direct, indirect, punitive, special, incidental or other consequential damages arising directly or indirectly from use of this material. Use of this material is provided as is and with no warranties.

HEALTH AND WELLNESS DISCLAIMER

This book is for educational purposes only. It does not provide medical advice. Information found on the Mind Rewire site is meant to motivate you to make your own health care and dietary decisions based upon your own research and in partnership with your healthcare provider.

The content is not intended to be a substitute for professional medical advice, diagnosis, or treatment. Always seek the advice of your physician or other qualified health provider with any questions you may have regarding a medical condition. Never disregard professional medical advice or delay in seeking it because of something you have read on this site. Reliance on any information provided by Mind Rewire, others appearing in this book at the invitation of Mind Rewire is solely at your own risk.

FREE STRATEGY SESSION

Because everyone is different and has faced different challenges in their lives,

I created Mind Rewire sessions to help on a personal level.

But-

If you want to learn how to rewire your mind on your own- go to

https://MINDREWIRE.com

And you can get the course that will give you the directions and methods I use.

If that personal touch is what you want then look on the home page for the button that looks like this-

If you knew you could direct your thoughts and beliefs so that they pushed toward the future and released you from the past wouldn't you want to do that, and learn how so that you never get stuck in the same place again?

TABLE OF CONTENTS

CHANGE

The other day, I was reading a book that a friend of mine wrote, called *The 21 Day Miracle*. In the first part of the book, he asks this question: "Do you want to know the biggest lie in personal growth?" He goes on to tell the story of the tortoise and the hare, and notes that people are always told that slow and steady win the race; in other words, persistence and consistency create champions. In reality, he says, this is simply not the case. Put a real rabbit next to a real tortoise in a race and see what happens.

Stories like these stretch the truth in certain ways to make people see what the storyteller wants them to see. The story has been told so many times that it starts to seem like the truth. Nobody ever really challenges the story or the idea that it teaches because it has become a staple life message. The same is true of any story, whether it's your own or one that somebody else has told you.

If a story becomes a belief, that belief will eventually become your reality.

Thinking again about the tortoise and the hare, how many times have you heard that story, or that slow and steady will win the race? On the surface, it makes sense. But how many goals have you worked towards slowly and steadily, yet never achieved anything?

Reflecting on all of my clients and their various issues, I realized that one of the bigger problems that stands out is procrastination. This is a problem that almost everybody I work with talks about at some point or another. I hear about it from people across all walks of life and from many countries, and after reading my friend's book, it made me wonder just how many of those people had worked on their issues slowly and steadily. How many of them had heard that story as children and determined that slow and steady win the race? The truth is that, while persistence and consistency can indeed help people achieve great things in life, if there's a rabbit standing next to you and you're the tortoise, you're probably going to lose.

What would happen if you started moving like the rabbit and carried out your movements with purpose and meaning? What would this change in your life? This is what my program, Mind Rewire, is designed to achieve. It's how I help people rewire their minds and change their thinking to align with the things they want in their lives. It's what happens when you start a process with the deliberate intention of changing the circuitry of your brain.

What if you could create what you want in your life? What if you could walk away from your past experiences and emotions and create something brand new – start becoming that thing, that dream? Can you become your dream? Do you think it's possible? It is, and I want to teach you how.

I wrote this book because, at the end of the day, after all I have done and learned, I know that the subconscious mind and the human ability to hold onto negative things will stall out anyone's process.

I watched my life turn into a mess and had no idea that it was happening because of things in my subconscious mind. We live in a world full of so much negativity, and the rate the negativity spreads seems to be getting faster and faster. It is infectious and easy to get caught up in.

The negative feelings, thoughts and emotions become like a skin. They feel normal, and even though we may not like it, they are comfortable to us. Feeling good on a consistent basis is abnormal and can even feel taboo. What would you do to feel good on a more consistent basis?

This negative nature does not only come from our attitudes and perceptions. It is a part of the environment we live in. It also comes from pollution, the air quality, the quality of the food we eat, and the quality of the water we drink.

When we become ill, we have a tendency to seek blame. We blame our family, our parents, our genes, others around us in our toxic environments — maybe your diet, the doctor and a misdiagnosis (or missed diagnosis). Some of us even blame God, or decide that there isn't a higher intelligence because one would never let His creation get to the point of a destructive physical illness.

I wrote this book because of the negative cocktail of people and environmental influences of this world – from the ideals and concepts present in my immediate family to the attitudes of my distant relatives and the genetic misconceptions, such and the "hereditary" diseases I was supposed to get and was told I was born with.

My story starts with the realization that I don't remember my childhood. This realization came from a therapist who asked me to talk about mine over 12 years ago while trying to get to the bottom of the issues that were emerging in my life.

When he asked me to tell him about my childhood and I told him I didn't really remember it — and didn't care — he looked at me kinda weird and said, "Well, there is a red flag." I didn't know what he meant, or why that would be a red flag. He kindly explained to me that people do remember their childhoods, and sometimes with great detail.

All I could think was that when I looked into mine, all I could see was blackness. It was effectively blotted out — and apparently with just cause, according to sibling testimony.

At the apex of my demise, my health was failing. At 38, I had hormone issues, blood sugar issues, skin cancers, and what a doctor said was thyroid problems later called Hashimoto's. I had killed a bone in my foot for no apparent reason, and lost part of my gastrocnemius muscle in the process of fixing my foot during four surgeries. I was told by the doctor that discovered I didn't remember my childhood that I needed to go to a doctor who could prescribe, because he suspected bipolar disorder. And while the worry was the symptoms, no one, including the Psy.D, was overly concerned with my past than I was. And I wasn't concerned at all.

No one was asking about the inner turmoil that I couldn't really put a finger on, my childhood that was a black hole, or what was going on with my children in our home and the relationships there.

We had an older daughter who was way above average in multiple dimensions and seemed to excel at everything with great ease. A son who seemed to take the blow for all of the family's issues. He had a multiple congenital birth issues, including a co-arctation of the aorta and hip dysplasia. The heart issue was caught quickly and left other issues in its wake that no one could diagnose. No one, pediatricians, therapists, schools, or anyone else caught the hip issue that lead to a lifetime of what had to have been unimaginable physical pain. My son's array of misunderstood actions and reactions were misdiagnosed and mistreated by every doctor he saw and family members alike. His heart issue was not the big problem anymore, but because of complications, his brain took a hit that had unknowingly turned into the biggest issue. Because of the anoxia and blood gas accumulation, he was left with what a neuropsychologist later diagnosed as looking like a blunt force trauma to his frontal lobe. It left him with diagnoses like ADD, ADHA, bipolar, depression, and oppositional defiant disorder — all which were incorrect but left our household a mess. The hip dysplasia lead to a hip replacement at 17 years old, and pain that scarred his body and mind and every cell of his body.

The ups and downs of constant doctor visits and issues at home and at school were as easy to block out as my childhood. I was just going through motions.

Consequently, some of my diagnoses were not correct, either. A bipolar disorder misdiagnosis that left not only my body but my family in tatters.

Before medicating me, no one seemed to take into account that I didn't know the whole scope of my life, past or present. How could they? No one really knew, not even me. I was dealing with my son's issues in ways that only made them worse and dealing with my own from the perspective that they were there because my brain chemistry was off and they had nothing to do with the mayhem inside my house or the past I didn't remember.

All of the medication, diagnoses, and side effects caused more issues and misunderstandings than we, as a family, understood or knew how to deal with. And, at 300lbs, I knew something had to change. That is where my journey of learning how much power we humans really have begins.

✶   ✶   ✶

The intention of this book is to teach people how easy it is to start a process of change that will forever alter their lives. Becoming aware that something isn't right isn't enough.

If you feel like you are fighting against something invisible and can never seem to solve the issues at hand, there could be an issue caught in your subconscious mind. Maybe it was left over from an incident, a period of time or something someone said to you that wasn't even your problem, but you never shook it off.

Just like many of my clients, you have probably tried everything. You tell yourself a thousand good things and never see lasting change, and your meditation practice seems to fall flat. And everything you try seems like it's working at first, but then you end up back where you were and are ready to give up.

Mind Rewire will help you change by using the mechanisms that are already part of your system. It will teach you how take those affirmations and mantras that you say over and over to yourself and translate them into change on a subconscious level.

It is the way your system was made to work.

I teach this stuff all the time and bring release to people who say they have tried everything. They have done things like Reiki, Eft, NLP, talk therapy, meditation, yoga and breathing practices, but either can't do it, or don't stick with it long enough to see the changes they so desperately want. I always giggle, compassionately, when people tell me they even walked on fire and are so confused as to why they are still fighting the same issues.

Now, don't get me wrong: there is a ton of value to all of those things. I use some of these methods myself. But, most of the time, what I've found is that they don't get to a level deep enough to alter the thing that is causing you to feel stuck.

This book will help you understand why you feel stuck…

…why you say things to yourself that you don't mean, or that make no sense.

…why you have endless arguments in your head that have no winner and that wear you out.

…why you are sick and can't seem to heal no matter what you do.

…why years of therapy helped minimally if it helped at all, and why the doctors you have to believe in may only be making matters worse.

I am going to show you an easy way to start healing the system from different avenues that will quickly allow you to gain ground in an otherwise uncertain jungle of misguided attempts. These statements may seem bold, but it is what I did for myself and countless others who come to me for help and guidance.

The journey starts here. Are you ready for the ride? Be BOLD!

Finally, a note of gratitude:

I am thankful for all the people in my life who were strong enough to tough it out and hear the apologies and love me regardless. To the people who loved big enough to forgive and allowed forgiveness. To the people I lost and pushed away, I can only hope that someday you will allow me to try to say sorry and begin again.

I'm grateful for my beloved husband, without whom I wouldn't have survived, and also to my amazing son, who allowed me to practice my techniques and new ideas on him whenever I needed to (without too much of a fight). Also to my little brother, who continues to allow me to do the same…

They are an amazing testament to healing and being stronger than the things you come up against in this life.

I'm grateful for my lovely Emily, who consistently reminds me that I am enough.

To my dearest Meaghan, Kendal, Debbie, Bobbi, Nicole, Linda, Cynthia, Elma, and numerous other beautiful sisters and friends, without whom the journey would not have been possible.

To one of my favorites- Brian Lewis, Possibly the best coach I know- The most caring, compassionate, and patient person. I know you have heard it a thousand times, but I appreciate you and your family (Jane, Boden, and Londyn) more than words can ever say. Perception is everything. Your family showed me a different way to see!

And lastly, to one young lady who I can only hope knows how much she is loved and cared about. All I can do is wait for a change and to talk. That right was revoked years go after crazy issues that made no sense and that I still don't understand, to this day. For my part in the story, I am deeply sorry. I didn't know why I was reacting the way I was, and I followed advice that was very wrong. I can't explain it here, but when you are ready, I am open to a chance to listen and understand the things you never got to say out loud. I am forever grateful to you. Without your actions, none of this would be happening. I was able to stretch and learn and push boundaries I wouldn't have otherwise… and I have seen that you have, too! Denise, I love you.

Chapter **One**

WHY DO I NEED TO REWIRE MY MIND?

If you Change your beliefs you can change your life.

– Dr. Bruce Lipton

Rewiring is simply a way of renewing your mind and bringing it into alignment with the things that you want in life. It involves changing the beliefs that you have about yourself and the world around you. If your beliefs and thoughts are out of alignment, life can become a struggle.

People often come to me and say things like:

"I never get it right."

"I'm not good enough."

"I don't understand."

"I can't." "I don't."

"I hate myself."

They'll give me lists of thoughts that they have and we'll go through them together, one at a time, bringing them into the light. You would think most people already know this, but some don't. Some people simply hear and repeat the words to themselves over and over, not realizing that they're acting and reacting in their daily life according to the things they're thinking.

Along with these thoughts comes a bundle of emotions that have been accumulated from groups of feelings or body sensations. When you have a feeling, you probably have bodily sensations that go along with it, such as your heart beating harder or faster, your muscles twitching, or a chilly kind of tension somewhere. Emotion is the sum of all of these different feelings that you have, both internally and externally around your body, and to which you assign the name of an emotion.

How do you think when you feel a certain way?

What thoughts come into your mind when you're feeling a certain emotion?

When you think these thoughts, are you believing them to be true?

How do you live according to those beliefs?

You can only accept thoughts that are equal to the emotion you are in. For example, if what you are feeling is fear, you're going to be thinking about something that directly causes fear. Fear the emotion comes with set of sensations that help you remember the physical body position of that emotion. What does the body posture of fear look like? For some, submitting to the posture that is fear will remind the body to go into that chemical place and start the thoughts and actions that will go with it.

I can tell you about a time in my teenage years when I was on a roller coaster ride at a city park in our hometown with my brothers, and this roller coaster had huge dips and turns. People were laughing as if they were having fun, which they probably were, but what I didn't realize at the time was that the issues I had with heights and fast-moving objects would be an issue on this ride. My brothers and I all got on the roller coaster and I immediately began to feel the emotions that I was about to go through. My heart started racing and my head started pounding. My muscles were twitching, and I had a nervous sensation inside my stomach. As the roller coaster started going up and down, I felt not only fear, but panic. I was certain in those moments that I was going to die. I remember going through tunnels on the roller coaster, praying, literally yelling to God that I would be good for my whole life if I came out the other side and still had my head and limbs attached. I was thinking thoughts that were equal to the emotion I was feeling. To this day, thinking about a roller coaster makes me feel sick… I guess I should rewire that!

Some of the work that I do now will take people on a roller coaster ride. We'll feel emotions, become aware of thoughts and beliefs, but then do something different... What happens if you change the emotional value of a thought?

The answer is that the thought itself will change. What if I had been on that roller coaster ride, and instead of thinking about coming out of the tunnels and going up and down the hills and valleys, that sick feeling in my stomach getting worse, I had been thinking about something more positive?

What would have happened if I had been thinking about, oh, I don't know, having fun? My level of emotion would have been completely different. My thoughts would have been different.

The important thing to understand here is that the correlation between thoughts and emotions is enormous, no matter what you believe. A thought that you think will bring the emotion that goes with it into your system. The emotion brings the feelings and the feelings take you right back to the thought. Over time, these become beliefs.

As you keep going through the beliefs in your head, they start to define who you are and become your personality. When you get stuck in a loop or trail of negative thoughts that take you nowhere, it is imperative that you stop and remove it from your head. This is changing the circuitry that will help you change your life.

Rewiring your mind is something we do to change the circuitry. Renewing the mind is a practice, and something that you do on a daily basis. To keep the buildup out of your head and start living in the present, with a focus on being in alignment with your future, the practice becomes important. Positive or negative, you are constantly wiring something into your brain, and your life will reflect whatever that thing is.

Anything in your life that you want to change or achieve takes continuity, consistency, and persistence. However, while you can do this the slow, old-fashioned way, as in the story of the tortoise and the hare, or you can also choose to be like the rabbit and take the fastest route, which is what Mind Rewire does.

First, we're going to go through some of the methods that people use to try and change their experiences and emotions. We'll discover why some of them work and some of them don't, and then go into why Mind Rewire methods work as quickly as they do.

Dr. Joe Dispenza has said that your personality is a reflection of your personal reality. This is a beautiful way to say that if you have successfully rewired your mind, you'll no longer be the person you once were. You have to emerge a different person. If you're still doing the same things with the same emotions and the same beliefs behind them, the mind is not renewed; you are using the old circuits and you will remain the same person.

You have to slay the old you and take authority of your body and your brain, and then allow the new one to emerge. You have to sustain the new and keep walking in this new person to create the new circuits that will make it stick. The goal is to move things quickly and get yourself out of your own way to create real change.

I remember when we bought our first house. It was so awesome, and it had a two-car garage. When we first moved in, our garage was empty. There was space enough for two cars, plus some area to store things. As we started moving in, there was garden equipment and tools and other assorted things that were stored in this garage. A few boxes stacked neatly in a corner. But both cars could still fit.

As we lived there and continued to grow our family and collect tools, bikes, toys, animals, more tools, garden equipment... the garage got fuller.

After around five years, the garage was full enough that only one car could fit into it. There were boxes arranged and stacked so that I could still get my car in, but my lovely husband had to resort to parking in the driveway.

The stacks got higher and would sometimes fall over and either be re-packaged and stacked or just pushed as deep into a corner as they could be and left. Eventually, something would get positioned on top and the thing underneath would get forgotten.

Before long, my car almost wouldn't fit. I would pull in and squeeze out of the door as to not scrap the paint. Once in a while, I would go out and try to sort things and restack them to make it easier to get my car in.

Have you ever driven down a street and seen an open garage that was so packed to the edge with boxes and stuff that you think, "Oh my gosh! I'm so glad that's not mine..."

If you've ever had a similar experience, you might not even remember when you started stacking things in the garage. What was even in those boxes? What is in the next layer deep? Would it be worth getting rid of the stuff that is filling your space and not doing any good?

This is kind of the same idea as your brain. As a baby, you started out brand new and clean. Nothing there but love and space to grow. Depending on what you were taught and what you held onto, you started to form ideas about yourself and the world around you.

That little person was spotless and clean, but as life unfolded and things happened around you, you were filled up with ideas, thoughts and beliefs and you never released — things that should not have been yours to carry around to begin with.

You were filled with (mis)information that God never wanted you to have. What would life have been like if you had been given information that would have allowed you to fight and be strong against the adversities of life?

7

What would life have been like if you had known how loved and loveable you really are? What would life have been like if someone had spoken words that constantly refilled and nurtured you, instead of letting you down, making you feel bad, and causing you pain? In order to be in the present, you have to be able to let go of the past.

Think about New Year's resolutions. They are a very interesting thing. The whole purpose of a New Year's resolution is to get yourself set up to be in the present moment, to start something new, to walk away from the old things that you didn't like about yourself. To move out of things that aren't helping you thrive or helping you gain momentum in your life.

But, a lot of times, we start New Year's resolutions or a new project, a new day even, with the same old thought processes. We have a new idea, but the same thoughts and the same emotions come up against us. It's the same old things that tends to trip us up. Being able to form a new thought process and have a new emotional value to hold onto it becomes a really interesting idea.

When you're stuck in the same old thoughts, the same old ideas, the same old memories, the same old beliefs, year after year, you'll find yourself wasting time doing the same things and fighting against yourself to do it differently. It may be time to sit down and start asking questions. Start to listen to yourself and know what is being said inside your head. What are your thoughts saying to you? Do you even know?

8

This seems to be the game that we've tried to play with ourselves as a human race for a very long time. How do you walk away from the old stuff? How do you embed new thoughts and emotions into yourself, into your existence, into your life, and come out a whole different person?

This is what I work on with different people, all the time. They come to me for all different kinds of reasons, from different backgrounds, from ethnicities, and with different needs. They say they have tried everything. Some of them are at the end of their rope. But, they all have a common problem. There are neuropathways in their brain that keep giving them the same information.

The information, just like the stuff in the back of the garage, was at one point good stuff. It was useful. But now, some 15, 20, 30 years later, that stuff is a nuisance sitting in your garage, and you have either forgotten it is there, or you just don't want to clean it up. The idea of it wears you out and you don't even consciously think of it, you just know you are tired.

So, let's do a little exercise. I want you to think about the questions that you ask yourself. We tend to ask ourselves the same questions over and over. Maybe they are questions like, "What do I want out of my life? What is my life's purpose?" Maybe you're asking yourself things like, "Why me? Why can't I have that?" or "What am I doing wrong?"

Being able to formulate a different question that would yield a different result would sound something like, "What am I doing to get myself into a position that will give me the result that I want?" The action itself will start to create a different process. It will create a different mindset.

Can you become aware of what you are telling yourself?

What if that doesn't work?

If you can't get there, this is where you notice that feeling of being stuck. It may actually be a total blind spot, and you have absolutely no idea why. You don't even see it. You just know you can never get anywhere. You're not making it through to the things that you want to do.

We talk about it like it is a road block. People will try different things all the time. We've used things like meditation, affirmations, tapping, NLP... all of these different tools and tricks. Even inside a psychologist's office, they use different ideas. I worked with a psychologist once that did a form of prayer meditation. I've done EMDR, brain spotting, EFT... These types of protocols can actually be super helpful.

But **if** it doesn't get to the underbelly of the issue and pull apart and release the things that cause you to be stuck **and** (and this is very important), **implant ideas that will actually work for you and work with you,** you won't see the changes you want.

If you're engaging in old habits, if you're always bringing up the same old issues and rehashing what happened yesterday, what happened when you were a kid... if you're reliving in your subconscious the hurtful things that someone told you... maybe it's something a doctor told you... a parent... someone at school... then you are going to keep going in the same direction. If that makes you feel stuck, that is where you will stay.

It's a function of your brain to hold and store pictures, ideas, and emotions about what happened to you during the course of your life. And if those things weren't positive, if they weren't something that'll actually benefit your life, you will end up with a feeling that you might be able to describe. But, that leaves you moving in cycles and circles, going over and over the same patterns that don't help you, and they don't benefit you in the walk that you want to be on.

If you want to do things differently, the first step has to be to get underneath all of that and clean out your subconscious storage locker. Maybe that's the first right question to ask: **How do I clean out my subconscious mind?**

Your life is the sum of things you have stored. You are defined by this. It can be stagnant, painful, and cause illness. But, it should not be that way Your life should be a sum of the things you are. Currently. Now. Ever changing, growing, expanding, and flowing.

Your future is about what you want. Hopes, dreams, de-sires.

Use this link and go to Mind Rewire
to check out my course

https://www.mindrewire.com/programs

Chapter **Two**

HOW POWERFUL IS THE MIND?

Your Personality creates your personal reality.

— *Dr. Joe Dispenza*

What are beliefs? Put simply, a belief is an idea that you think to be true about yourself, or about someone else, or even about the world around you. Your belief could be about something you should have learned, heard, or understood about yourself, but for whatever reason you failed to do so. Whether this belief is true or false, good or bad, it is created when something happens to you.

Beliefs are formed when you learn something, witness something, have someone tell you something, and dedicate time and emotion to it by thinking about it.

If you're treated a certain way or treat yourself a certain way, you are creating beliefs. These can easily come from everyday life situations — things that happen around you. Beliefs can cause horrible lifelong issues or wonderful outcomes. They can cause intense, miraculous healings and quick, certain deaths.

I want you to stop and get quiet for a moment now, going deep within yourself to ask this question: What do you tell yourself?

What are the things that you hear yourself saying and thinking? Ask if they are really true. Write down your answers. This is good information to have. It is a way to start a process of becoming aware of your internal dialogue.

While you write these things down, I want you to think for a second about the idea that your thoughts actually have some role to play in the way you live your life. Do you ever wake up in the morning and actively work on creating a better future for yourself? Have you ever worked with yourself on such a level that you truly create what you want in your mind and see the fruit of it in your life? Are you willing to strive for it, day in and day out?

Can you start the process by thought alone?

Most people don't participate in a practice like that daily, often because they don't believe it to be true. But we see evidence of this all the time. Notice the people around you and the lives that they live. What are the things they complain about the most, and what are the things that they actually do the most? How do they live their lives? How do they function? What do you notice about the things they are thinking and speaking about, and how do their actions match up?

A person who is always saying "I'm going to get sick" spends a lot of time being sick. A person who has an accident or illness that caused pain and then talks about the pain a lot, stays in pain longer than a person who actively does something to counter it.

More importantly, it's interesting to note how easily things could be altered if they just said some things a little differently. If you knew beyond all reasonable doubt that your thoughts created your experience and your reality, would you ever waste a day ruminating on everything that passed through your mind? If you were absolutely sure that you could consciously create the future that you see, would you ever let any thought slip by your awareness that you didn't want active in your life?

How powerful are you? Thoughts create action inside your body. Thoughts create action in our reality. Here is an example-

Whenever I feel like I am going to catch a cold, I start talking to my body about killing the virus or bacteria. I talk to my system and tell it to activate the necessary healing response that will keep me feeling well. I rarely get sick to a point that I can't stop.

I want you to think for a moment about a baby being born. This tiny human being is spotless, with no beliefs save that he will be loved and taken care of, because that's what has happened the entire time he was inside the womb. There are no issues for the baby to deal with. He or she is fine until someone looks at him or her and says, "Look where you are or where you will never be." People are constantly told things about themselves that aren't true and yet own them anyway, and assign them an emotional value. They then become beliefs that people live by because they don't know any better. I have a friend that tells her son every time he sneezes or coughs that he is getting sick- he walks around repeating I'm getting sick, and guess what , he does, every time.

I want to tell you a little about my story and how I grew up. I grew up with a mother who was sick. She seemed very troubled and was also, unfortunately, something of a hypochondriac. She was always sick, always struggling with one illness or another, having constant surgeries and things going wrong inside her body. If there was nothing going wrong, she would invent something. She would go to a doctor and they would find something wrong, give her something else to look at or think about, a new reason to operate. These surgeries were usually exploratory and would give her a lot of attention. All eyes would be on her until she was healthy, and then it would start all over again.

As a child, I was always wondering when the same thing would start happening to me. My mother was sick and overweight, and I was petrified of growing up to be like her. As a junior high school kid, fought against this idea by contradicting her at all times. If my mother said something was blue, I would say it was white. If she said it was big, I would try and explain why I thought it was small. Nothing in our house ever seemed to make sense, and that's exactly what I knew about life. It didn't make sense. It was a hard way to live and I hated myself for it, because it was a struggle that I couldn't understand and didn't know how to fix. Over time, these thoughts turned into my core beliefs. They were thoughts that I carried around for years inside my head as I was coming into the world as a young adult. The words that I heard myself saying were:

"This is hard."

"This is confusing."

"I hate myself."

"Nothing makes sense."

I said these things over and over again. As I grew into a young adult, these beliefs were turning into fruit in my life. Looking back, I can see the evidence everywhere.

What are your core beliefs, and how are these beliefs limiting you? Take your pencil and start writing. What are the core beliefs that you hear yourself repeating? Can you pick them out? In what ways are they keeping you locked away from the things you want to do – the things you dream about and that you truly want for your life?

As far as my mother goes, she has changed greatly over the course of the few years. As her illness became worse and worse, she suddenly started finding a way to emerge from the depths and is now a completely different person. I will always wonder what her core beliefs were, what she herself was told as a child, what things became beliefs from the farm she grew up on or what words the doctor said to her that became her reality.

I'm not sure what she did that finally started the process of change for my mother, but I know what mine was. It was a knock on death's door after I had gained so much weight that I was all but exploding at the seams. I was around 300 pounds. A great family friend had passed away from cancer and nothing seemed to be going right in my life. The doctor told me that if I didn't start changing things, it would probably be the end of me, and so I set out on this journey to figure out what it was that was causing the bulk of my issues.

Weight was the obvious and so I began my journey inside a gym. I started working out. I started doing things differently, as far as eating was concerned. I started a process that helped to peel the weight off a little at a time – but the greatest change occurred when I finally realized that what I was thinking was so negative and so hard to listen to that nothing else was going to change if I didn't change that. I remember the very day when I was sitting on a spinning bike inside a gym in Centennial, Colorado, hating myself and the words going around inside my head. As I plopped myself down in front of a mirror, all of a sudden in the back of my head I heard the words, "I love you."

I jerked around, thinking that someone was behind me. There was no one there. And as I sat there, I looked in the mirror in front of me and I remember thinking to myself, "Hey, you're kind of cute." I had never heard or said those words to myself before. I was about 40 years old and that was the first time I had ever heard myself say the words "I love you" to me.

It's an interesting conversation to go over with the clients I have now. Can you look at yourself, say "I love you," and mean it? More importantly, do you have the feeling of the emotion that you can attach to those words when you say them about yourself? If you don't, it's one of the places to start from as we begin to build a foundation that will help you find emotion and be able to attach it to the future that you want for yourself.

This is the kind of situation I see most often with clients: You have an event. Something happens that causes an experience where chemicals are suddenly released into your body. If it's a bad experience, these are chemicals such as cortisol and adrenaline which cause stress or fear. If it's a good experience, the chemicals are oxytocin, serotonin, dopamine, and other neurochemicals associated with good feelings. With either of these types of chemicals comes the physical sensation.

You have a feeling going on inside your body during this event or experience, and after it's over, as things begin to clear out, you sit down somewhere and think about what just happened. If you think about it hard enough, you can actually pull up the emotion again. You feel it, which means those chemicals are coming back into your system and creating circuitry inside your brain. You're actively creating a loop of neuroplasticity, and inside that loop are the chemicals that give you a feeling. The more you think about it, the more you build circuits. You sit inside that event or experience, thinking that thought and feeling those emotions, until it becomes a belief.

That belief is a perception about yourself, somebody else, or the world around you, and because of that perception, you start reacting differently to your environment. You live your life according to the chemical construction that your body and brain had sent out during that original event. You might try and think about that event differently, but the chemical relation remains the same and so you experience that chemical relation over and over again. This all becomes a belief about yourself, and it is through this perception that you live your life. And you are stuck…

This is how dreams are crushed. It's also how dreams can be magnified and built. Think about it for a minute. If your core beliefs are that you hate yourself and life is hard, what kind of existence do you think you're going to have, even when something is actually easy and you have the ability to do it well?

Looking back, it's interesting to me how hard I made some of the simplest things. I had friends telling me that it was called self-sabotage. This sabotage was directly linked to the fact that I thought that life was hard, and that nothing made sense. Because I thought that so often and would actually sometimes verbalize it, it had eventually turned into a hardwired silent thought in my subconscious. It was the truth of my reality.

Personal, private sessions to create a new reality-
Mind Rewires Core program is designed to get you clear of subconscious stress-
With the quickness and ease that you want and deserve.
To speak to me privately go here, this is the direct link to book-
https://meetme.so/mindrewire

Book your strategy session today.

Chapter **Three**

UNDERSTANDING THE MIND, SUBCONSCIOUS ISSUES, AND AUTOMATIC REPONSES

"Whatever we plant in our subconscious mind and nourish with repetition and emotion will one day become a reality."

— *Earl Nightingale*

We talked about events and experiences and how they express chemicals into your body that we relate to emotions.

You have feelings inside of your body that correspond to these emotions, and along with the event or experience they create a memory.

In turn, that memory becomes something you think about over and over until eventually it becomes a belief and you start to form actions around it.

From these beliefs come perceptions about yourself and the world around you, and you start living your life according to this memory and chemical construction. In this way, your bodies are directly linked to the original event or experience and the chemical concoction that your body gave you in that given moment.

Oddly this can happen even when you don't remember a thing.

I have plenty of people who come in saying, "I have a feeling. I don't know why I feel this way. I don't remember much of my childhood, so I don't really know where it comes from."

I've had this experience myself. Here is what I know now.

The brain is a storage locker. It saves these events, whether you remember them or not. It harnesses the emotion by the chemical concoction excreted into your system at the time to keep track of what exactly occurred. When something starts happening around you, your brain will begin searching for something inside to relate it to, and it will send you back whatever is found that resembles it with emotional value.

This is equivalent to your subconscious mind. Your subconscious mind is said to be made up of 95% of your daily thought activity. In other words, only 5% of your daily thought activity comes from the conscious mind, or the things you're actually aware of. Those events and experiences, with their chemicals and related emotions, are stored in the subconscious mind, in a place that you're not even aware of. If you are living by memories and emotions because of chemicals and hormones kicking up in your system and they are not in alignment with the thing you are trying to do in that moment, you will notice a problem. This is when people will fight, struggle, or even quit a project or dream and say that they are just not good enough to do it.

Here is an example. Your name is a very important piece of who you are. It's how you recognize yourself and how other people recognize you, not only verbally but also visually. Think about it — with the sound of your name not only comes an auditory signal but also a visual one. There are also feelings, emotions, memories, ideas, and beliefs associated with the sound of your name. I have worked with many people at this point, both men and women, who, when we start testing their system, find that they react strongly to the sound their own name. When your name signals stress in the system, it's the first thing we need to clear. These people usually feel heart palpitations, pain, or that old gut feeling that something awful is about to happen.

The name issue is always one that stems from childhood. The person may have come from a family that used his or her name as a kind of weapon. The stress created in the system was not addressed and, over time, built up into a big problem. You automatically respond to the chemicals created from a childhood issue.

The good news is that if your name is an issue, clearing it is very simple. It's as easy as sitting and thinking about your name, saying it repeatedly in your head while holding your body in a Whole Brain State until the issue releases and your perception changes. I do this constantly as a part of my work, and it's interesting how much can change when that single issue is cleared.

If you think about that for a minute, hearing the sound of your name and having it cause a negative visceral reaction can really screw with your life.

One woman I worked with spent an entire session just on her own name. She was a school secretary and heard her name called all the time. Staff members and students would come into her office, always starting what they were about to say by speaking her name. That sounds reasonable. They always wanted something from her. That sounds reasonable, too; after all, she was the secretary. Because of her position and the constant bombardment of hearing her name, her issues grew progressively worse until she could no longer stand the sound of her name, and she started thinking things like:

"I just want to kill everybody."

"I'm so tired of being in the office."

"I hate my job."

"I hate my life."

"Everything is a mess."

That sounds really bad, but it is what stress does. The more it happened, the more it piled up in her system and the more tense she got. She knew there was a problem; she knew it was getting worse. She just didn't know what was causing it or why she felt this way. Once we started working together, she recognized that in her childhood, there was an incident that contributed to this. It had the same feeling to it that she got whenever her name was called.

Once we worked to get rid of this tension and the resistance to hearing the sound of her name, she reported to me in less than a day and a half that everything was very different. She could now sit in her office and be at peace. I left her with some tools to keep her clear of negative energy for herself and her workspace, and to work with the people who were coming in and out of her office, so that they understood that they were not allowed to bring their negative energy inside. She had to learn how to have a conversation about what was going on, as well as to make sure that her name was clear of any resistance so that when people said it, she could sit calmly and get through whatever was necessary.

Her resistance to her name came from something that had happened when she was much younger. She was surprised to learn in the course of our work that when she said her own name, the pit of her stomach felt like it was rising up into her throat. She told me that it shocked her to realize it made her feel that way — but it was the exact same way it made her feel while in her office all day long. This was a huge clue that there was a problem in her subconscious.

Subconscious stress can affect your life in many ways, and for my client, it meant that simply hearing her own name spoken repeatedly made her not want to go in to work. It messed up her ability to get her job done and to do so efficiently.

My past

For me, the subconscious stress of saying "I hate you" and thinking that everything was hard had turned my whole life upside down. From working with a my own child who had huge emotional and physical struggles, to working in a household with chores that had to be done and working full-time as a pastry chef where I had to keep moving regardless of what was going on around me, it was always a struggle. The subconscious stress piled up until I had no idea what was going on. My automatic response was to get quiet and move faster. To try to hide while doing what I needed to. Or to shut down and not do anything. My life was a mess.

Subconscious stress can come from many different places, as does stress in general. Both can come from the environment, your experiences, your repeated thoughts, and even your imagination. However, there is a difference between them.

Stress vs. Subconscious Stress

I meet people every day who exhibit symptoms of stress. The interesting thing is that while they often talk about these symptoms, about half of the time, they don't even realize that they're stressed to begin with. It's quite common for people to be stressed and yet not understand that the body is actually doing a good thing by letting them know.

However, physically, this results in negative issues such as patterns of illness and disease. In homeopathic medicine and many other holistic health practices, stress is recognized as being able to causes imbalances within the body. When stressed, some parts of the body work overtime while others shut down completely.

Here is a list I found on an Ayurvedic practitioner's website of 10 signs that you can look for to recognize subconscious stress:

1. You have become more forgetful than usual.
2. You have irritable bowel syndrome (IBS) or heartburn.
3. You frequently get tension headaches.

4. You develop muscle twitches, especially in the eye area.

5. You have become irritable and your temper flares quickly.

6. You are not sleeping well at night.

7. You seem to be sleeping well but are always exhausted anyway.

8. You have trouble focusing on only one thing at a time.

9. You have high blood pressure.

10. You often get sick as a result of a weak immune system.

If you are exhibiting one or more of these stress signals, it's a good idea to discuss stress and stress management with your doctor or other qualified health professional.

So, how do we know if our stress stems from the subconscious or from everyday stressors? There's no definitive test, but subconscious stress is very often formed in a traumatic childhood — for example, having parents who were angry and stressed themselves, having basic physical or emotional needs not consistently met, or just living in generally bad conditions.

A great many people I talk to say that they had good childhoods, but also have some issues that persist 15 or more years later, with symptoms that didn't make sense. This makes a good case for having an ongoing practice to help take care of issues and stress. It's a good reason to take care of the brain and keep it cleaned out, get rid of old subconscious clutter by constantly doing things that revitalize and renew your mind on a daily basis.

It could be that even that though your childhood was generally fine, there was just one small, impactful event. Maybe you fell from a horse, witnessed a tragedy, or heard angry and unkind words. Maybe you were a part of something that, as a child, you had no words or explanation for that you now have to reckon with as an adult.

I like to describe subconscious stress as something you can't quite put your finger on, or have no real reason for. You may lack a way to properly explain the place you find yourself in or the way you feel in a situation. These things create patterns or cycles that are hurting you and hindering your progress in life.

I know for sure that physical issues stem from subconscious stress when people come to me saying that they have worked and worked on this thing and it doesn't ever seem to go away because they can't get it to release. When there is seemingly no explanation, I can tell that the problem is a subconscious one. Remember, most therapy protocols work from a standpoint of the conscious mind.

Medicine generally works from a standpoint of symptoms. Medicine seeks to cover the issue, not address the original issue. It's like you are trying to convince yourself of something other than what you are really feeling. It's an entirely different matter when you can release issues from the subconscious and feel the difference and see the evidence in your life...

A good example of this is a man that came to me asking, "If I say 'I'm calm and confident' when I am not, the mind has conflict. And that's not good, so what do I do?" This is like using an affirmation. Affirmations are useless, unless said many, many times, and generally only hit on the level of your conscious mind. And while it can make you feel good and positive in that moment, it doesn't stick in the subconscious — you didn't grow new circuitry.

At one point this man took medicine to relieve the discomfort of this issue, over time the issue got worse and had bigger ramifications due to side effects of the prescribed.

The conflict is inside his brain, he lived through something in his young life that gave him the pathways that say he is not calm or confident. It came with an emotional rush and, even now, has a feeling to it.

He took this on as truth and created a belief. The circuits were built, and now it is a core belief. But he wants to be calm and confident. He says he sees other people who appear to be every day. Why can't he?

So, telling yourself something you either do not fundamentally believe or cannot produce evidence of in your life will only lead to conflict. This will persist until something happens that jolts you, or the subconscious is able to release and reset the information.

There are a few ways to do this easily. Meditation will get you there eventually. Hypnosis will get you there if you have a good practitioner. With a good heightened emotional state it will happen faster.

How Mind Rewire Sessions Work

With most people I work with, we dismantle the limiting belief. This is to tear down the lie, the thing that you believe. It's the belief you have been living by that is simply not true, but that you were told or learned and now act it out in your daily life.

The truth is that you could probably go through your life and point out places when you were calm and confident, but those places were fleeting and you never got a good chemical rush that made it stick. To make the change permanent, we then seed in the new information, then bring in a heightened emotion up to set it in place with the feel good chemicals in the system.

We have to teach the body a new way to feel in place of the old way of feeling that you have done for years. The old way will eventually cause disease and problems in the body.

Stress and issues that hinder your progress will keep you in the past instead of creating a great future and enjoying the present.

We must teach the body to find the new feeling and hold onto it and add new circuits that will allow you to continue to think differently. The new circuits are created when you imagine, dream, and decide to live a different reality.

How do I know it works?

The way we know is by experiential evidence. What fruit are you producing? What is happening in your life that shows you that difference? If there is no difference, no fruit, then I know we missed the mark. I have only seen that happen a couple of times.

At some point, you have to start telling the body want you want it to do. You have to command the actions necessary to take charge of your life. Step up and take control! Life is a pleasure and the world becomes your oyster when you command authority.

To take the Mind Rewire course online go to

https://www.mindrewire.com/programs/

Chapter **Four**

HOW TO CHANGE THE SUBCONSCIOUS MIND

I want you to think for a minute about what you've tried in the past. I have clients who tell me all the time that they take part in therapy and have done so for years, from cognitive therapy and talk therapy to things like hypnosis, meditation, NLP, EFT, LOA, constellation work, yoga… The list of affirmations that people come in with and say failed to take hold is almost mind boggling.

Clients have even told me about doing past life regressions. Just the other day, I had a woman say to me that she was told she had arrows in her from a previous life. She said that if another person told her that she has arrows in her back and wants to remove them for her, she was going to scream. She asked me what this meant. Was it a metaphor of some kind, or was it actually going to take place in reality? Were the arrows something that had happened in a past life and now turned into a subconscious issue?

All I could tell her was that while I didn't know anything for sure about past lives, we can come at these issues by taking apart the neuroplasticity to release some of the feelings to the issues locked inside. And remove the chemical association to the emotional attachment to the trauma. What we did was exactly that.

I asked her what it was that she was feeling and describing to these other practitioners that had them looking at arrows. Despite having no memory of the event itself, she had a feeling. By dealing with the feelings that arose from it and disassembling the chemicals associated with the feeling, she felt relief from the symptoms that she had been fighting for the last 40 years.

Now I want you to go through your mind and take a quick mental stock of all the things you've tried in the past. Which of these methods worked and which did not? Did some methods work only sometimes? What methods or protocols did you try that did absolutely nothing for you? These questions I ask when a person can't quite put their finger on an issue — when they have no real explanation for something and yet find themselves in repeating patterns that are hurting them, stopping them from making progress in life, and keeping them from their dreams.

So why do some protocols work well or for a little while and others don't work at all? The answer is that some of the methods you have tried don't work because they only target the conscious mind. Remember, the subconscious makes up only 5% of your daily thinking. If the protocols you're trying, such as writing affirmations or saying mantras, are only targeting your conscious mind, how many times do you think you have to repeat them to get them to stick?

The subconscious is activated when a tragedy happens, when something shocks you, or when your mind is open and a pattern that is receptive to waves allows new information to get in, such as when you are from zero to seven years old. The brain waves at that point are not what they are right now, in your adult head. It's a different chemistry and functioning. To get into the subconscious mind, we have to do something different.

Hypnosis is one of the biggest things people tend to think about in relation to this, but many people don't like hypnosis because they feel that it's intrusive and scary to give up their power and control. I know this because I've had a lot of people come to my door saying exactly that. They've tried hypnosis despite their fears and it didn't work for them. Is that a belief thing? I don't know. But I do know when they are relaxed and in control they get better results.

I've also had clients who were certified hypnotists themselves. They were trained in hypnotism and yet said it didn't work for them personally. I've had people ask me if it's a belief issue, and if that by itself is part of their problem because they can't believe in what it is that they are doing. I can't give a straight answer to that because it would be different for every single person.

What I do know is that if you are consciously aware of what's going on around you while we're changing your brain state and creating new circuitry, like I said before, you get better results. You're a real part of the change and the one who is actively doing it — that, by itself, makes a huge difference.

How does Mind Rewire Change the Subconscious?

To change the subconscious, I use a couple of different methods. One of them is targeted. By going in deep and allowing your alpha waves to come into coherence to an issue, we're trying to bring all of your thoughts, beliefs, and systems into alignment in that alpha coherence.

The other method I use is a whole brain state, and this seems to do the same thing rather quickly. It's a technique that I learned and have used in several different protocols. It's used in Comprehensive Energy Psychology, Splankna (a Christian protocol for mind-body psychology), Brain Integration Therapy, and Psych-K. Why does a whole brain state work? Because when you're crossing the midline of your body, your brain has to sort for stability. When we talk about muscles and their function, the second you cross the midline, your brain begins to look for which muscles to turn on and which to turn off in order to keep you stable and in the position that you're in, be it standing or seated.

It works the same way with memories, beliefs, and emotions. If we pull up an emotion, touch the edge of a memory, or talk about belief and then sit in a whole brain state, an issue can start to clear the patterns of your autonomic nervous system and move out of your subconscious mind. It's interesting to witness someone skeptical about this method, who says something like, "I don't believe in this" or "my faith isn't enough" sit there and watch their body in action while something clears their system quickly and easily. In fact, in most cases, it takes less than two minutes. The longest I ever saw it take was up to five minutes, although when pared down to using just a whole brain state and attaching it to the emotion, memory, belief, or issue, it seems to happen much quicker.

I talked about one of my beliefs at the beginning of this book – that we've made dealing with our issues a lot harder than it needs to be. I believe that the whole brain state is one of the body's natural reactions to clearing the system when a issue happens and chemicals are released and not needed over time..

Sadly, it's a reaction that we were actually taught not to do and not to use. Think back to when you were in high school. If you're around my age, you were born in the early or mid-60s, when one of the things taught to us in school was about body posture. We were told that if someone crossed their arms, it meant they were shutting themselves off and being standoffish.

In reality, what you're doing when you cross your arms is a very natural process. If something is confusing to you or not coming across well, people will often cross their arms and lean in as they try to get the gist of the situation. This is your brain in action as it processes what's going on before, after, and even during the situation. Crossing your legs seems to make this even more powerful, and so we sit and hold this specific posture, this crossover pattern, until the issue clears the system.

This is what I teach people: how to feel this in their system so that they know which way to cross and how it correlates to the issue, belief, or thought that we are working on at the time.

To begin to Rewire Your Mind in a fast, effective way, contact me here by scheduling a 30-minute strategy session and see if Mind Rewire is right for you.

Go to
https://meetme.so/mindrewire now!

Chapter **Five**

LIMITLESS

Neurons that fire together wire together. Let's take apart the wiring so they can't keep firing! (especially if you are firing things that limit your life)

This is a little exercise that I take people through whenever I'm working with them over Skype or in a zoom room. It teaches them how to feel the chemistry of their body and how it corresponds to what they're thinking and feeling.

First, I want you to sit with your feet flat on the floor and your arms on either side of your body, not crossed anywhere over your midline. As you're sitting there, do a quick body scan. The body scan is something you do just to feel your body and become aware of what you're feeling, whether it's physical or emotional. Start at the top of your head and scan down through your body with your eyes closed, breathing normally and taking notice of the sensations inside your body. Just notice what you're feeling and then write it down.

Take about two minutes to do this. There aren't any right or wrong answers here; it's simply whatever you're feeling — muscle twitches, pinches, pokes. You could be feeling your heartbeat, tension or pain, or an emotion of some sort. Just write down whatever you notice.

Then, **think of something that you like,** or that makes you feel good. You are accessing a memory with this. Bring it up into your conscious mind and really think about it. Feel it, know it, taste it, smell it. See the colors and hear the sounds. When you've got it, do a body scan and notice what you're feeling.

Write it down.

After you've done that, I'm going to have you do something to **contrast** that: **think of something you don't like** – something simple and easy that you don't have a huge emotional response to, like a certain food. Like the thing or the memory that made you feel good, really feel this one, too, and bring it up in your system until you can see, hear, touch, or taste it vividly. How does that thing you don't like make you feel inside your body? Now, compare the two things you just thought about, good and bad. How did your like feel, and how did your dislike feel? Write it down.

Most people report back to me that the positive thing felt expansive or uplifting. They use words like "carefree" and "freedom." Conversely, most people say that the negative thing gave them a sensation of being pushed down or pushed backwards, or like there's a pit in the bottom of their stomach or the energy was being drained out of their system. Remember, the point here is only to notice what the differences are for each thing or memory, nothing more. You can also do this with your own name. I tell people to say something like, "My name is..." and then note how their name makes them feel – uplifted or open or expansive, for example. Then, say a different name in place of your own and notice if there is a difference in your body.

What you're actually feeling are the chemicals coming into your system from something that you like, making you feel good. You get positive chemicals that are associated with the good feelings such as dopamine, serotonin, and oxytocin. On the other hand, the chemical released into your body when you think of things you dislike, such as cortisol and adrenaline, are preparing your system for a fight or flight response and make you feel tense.

Those negative chemicals are associated with subconscious stress. If the system is stressed about an issue, for example if a person says their own name and gets a surge of these kinds of chemicals in response, we know there is subconscious stress involved. This person could use a whole brain state to clear that issue up. Mind Rewire uses a whole brain state consistently in order to clear the issues that you're stuck with from your past, moving the chemical compilation of emotion away from the issue itself so that you no longer feel the emotions to the situation when it comes up in your system. And so, you also naturally stop thinking about it as much, and the emotion stops directing you back to the situation. As a result, the circuitry starts to come apart in your brain.

You may have heard the saying, "Neurons that wire together, fire together." Well, this is the undoing of that. If they are not firing together, they can't be wired together. They come apart, and you get freedom.

The longer you keep any given feeling in your system, the longer your body is giving you the chemicals and signals to your brain. If it feels good inside your system, this chemical construction is a signal to the brain that things are going right. You're not in fight or flight mode any more. For some, this feeling is so foreign that they are blown away what at relaxation feels like.

This is a great time to start to construct a future, to put something into play that you can look forward to, something that you want in your life, and to build whatever you have been dreaming of.

I worked with a woman in January 2018 who had gone to a school where nuns had hit her and left scars when she was in first grade. Her whole life, she wondered what she did wrong. At every turn, she was waiting to get hit for something. At 60 years old, she is worn out because of thoughts, feelings, and beliefs that in reality had nothing to do with her. After finishing one session, tears poured down her face.

She just kept repeating the word "relief". The relief must feel like glory and mercy to someone who has never felt it. It took less than 90 minutes to get her there. She is still enjoying the feeling months later.

What I need to take you through is a session to retrain your system and your brain to respond to different chemicals in a completely natural way. Instead of just repeating the old training where you respond to the negative chemicals your body has become used to, you get to feel different to a new thought that will allow you to see and move in a totally different way.

This is Mind Rewire, like affirmations and meditation on steroids. Your system learns fast, and locking in the new circuits to a new idea is a common result. The steroid is adding the chemical equivalent of emotion to the experience. You are retraining yourself how to feel…

How do I know? Experiential evidence. People just like you getting results in crazy short periods of time that blow them away. We are talking minutes. Generally, in a first session, we are walking backwards through time and speaking to the newly forming you. The infant inside the womb that is just coming to life. You get to speak words of life over the cells that didn't get the right information to start with. You speak over yourself the things you wish you had heard or knew to equip the adult you with information to feel good, be healthy, and succeed in this life.

People get to tell themselves and cradle themselves into a place of stability and health. They say things like, "I love you, you are good, you are amazing, you are brilliant, you are a genius, you are going to be okay, you are gifted, you are a bright light — full of hope, joy, happiness. You are a seed to the future." I had one man prophesying over himself, that he was going to be the one to change his generation and pull people out of poverty and make his area a place of prosperous movement and hope where there had been none. That's powerful as cellular information.

It's is what happened to me, the slow, old fashioned way. I fought and struggled and kicked myself through it. From a sick, overwhelmed mess to where I am now. Now, people call me their angel, tell me I'm blessed and gifted, that God favors me, that I'm counted among saints... I don't know about any of that, but what I do know is that the work I am doing creates changes quickly and speeds people into what they want and moves them lightyears faster than any therapy or doctor ever did.

What are you called to do? What would you want implanted into your cellular structure?

I get skeptics in all the time, who call me because I'm am trained in Psych-K, and they have been watching an old video of mine on YouTube. They have seen the videos before mine, Bruce Lipton's and Rob Williams', and they call me because I offer a solution that is clear and direct. But they do not believe it can be so easy.

You can go to my website and read the testimonials. My newest client, who on the phone told me that he doesn't have many issues and his childhood was good, bought a session anyway just to check it out, because he had heard so much about what this work was doing. In doing the preliminary work for the first session, he discovered that he had more things that he could clear up than he realized. Just from doing his homework, he became more aware and is excited to release things he previously thought were just his personality.

In a way, it's just like training a dog. You tell the dog to sit in the corner and every time he moves you need to remind him again to sit in the corner. For people, every time the old you comes back with the old chemicals, you have to remind yourself that this is not you. That you have moved away from that person. You have become a new person, new ideas, thoughts, and new mind.

With a whole brain state, your brain has to find stability and settle into a new pattern when you cross the midline of your body to a thought, a belief, or an emotion. And when you add a new, heightened emotion, you have to become a different person with different chemicals who does a different thing.

People may look at me and say that I'm crossing a boundary here and stepping out of line, claiming how easy this is to do when that has never been the case. I say let's clear your beliefs and the things you have learned that tell you it is supposed to be hard... and all I can say is this: try me.

Get on a call with me.

Do the work.

Give yourself some time each day to practice feeling how you want, and you'll see the difference!

Chapter **Six**

TALK THERAPY AND OTHER PROTOCOLS

As you read this chapter, keep in mind that I am not suggesting that you stop seeing your therapist. This is a major decision that can have far-reaching consequences and cannot be made lightly.

Why do so many people have trouble with talk therapy? Why do people spend year after year in an office with a doctor, hashing out the same issues over and over, yet never seem to get anywhere? While a few of them get lucky and gain the resolution they're looking for, many others walk away empty handed. That's what happened to me.

The same goes for many of the protocols out there for self-help. Some of them work consistently, while others don't seem to work at all. Some people get the benefit while others get nothing. I have had more than one person ask me, "Is it a matter of faith? Is my faith not enough, or is it just belief? Because maybe I don't really believe it will work?" Either or both of these could be true, but my guess is that it's more likely that the therapist or therapy or protocol just didn't quite hit the mark.

My experience with talk therapy was sitting for years in a therapist's office talking about the same issues, and him asking me the same questions as if they had been rehearsed. I ran through the same set of emotions time and time again, the tears running down my face as the drama unfolded but was never resolved in any meaningful or long-lasting way. It only sank deeper into the recesses of my brain. Talk therapy brought it up so that I thought about it constantly. I went home thinking about it. I woke up the next morning thinking about it.

None of the stuff we talked about was my forgotten childhood; because I didn't remember, it was never addressed. We simply went after the daily struggles and turmoil and kept the stress signals alive and well. The way in which neuroplasticity works is that the more you think about something, the more you build it up and the more you live it.

There are two things I learned from my therapist after sitting for so many years in his office. The first was to **keep your head on straight**. I'm pretty sure this man said that to me every single time I was there, and even now I still wonder what the heck it means. The other thing my therapist constantly told me was to **take the next step**. While that one made sense, towards the end of my time spent with him, I realized that taking the next step meant walking out of his office and never going back. The more I talked about my issues, the bigger those issues grew and the more messed up my life became.

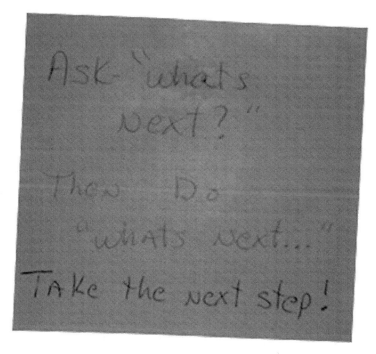

I have this note hanging over my desk to this day.

I started on a path of learning after that. I took courses and tested and learned everything I possibly could. Because of my faith and belief, one of the first things I learned was created by a Christian woman who called it Splankna. This utilized a lot of the techniques in energy psychology, such as

EMDR and EFT. She packaged it together with prayer and it was a powerful way to incite change. In this group, we were taught muscle testing, how to protect ourselves from dark energy, and that the body that God gave us was created to work a certain way and with a certain purpose.

However, the way your body works is through your mind, and what seems to happen is that unfortunately, over time, the body takes over. This is the same idea that Dr. Joe Dispenza teaches: the body has taken over in the cellular memory, which keeps you walking in the same direction you always have. It's only a matter of time before that cellular memory walks you into a hole that you can't come out of unless you do something to change it. It's not a matter of faith or how hard you believe, but simply the way your body works.

"You have to teach your body a new way to feel." – Dr. Joe Dispenza

Now, inside you, there's a system in place to effect the change necessary and alter your chemical construction, which not only effect your emotions but also your health. You can learn how to use that system to change the reality of the way you live.

It's about changing your mind and the energy of the emotional attachments and value that you've placed on things, raising it up to a level that's above the issue, circumstance, belief, and feeling itself. When you can do that, you will start to see the world itself change around you miraculously, seamlessly, easily – exactly the way your body and mind were created to make it do!

Go to

www.MindRewire.com

to see if rewiring your mind is right for you.

Chapter **Seven**

WE HAVE MADE THIS HARDER THAN IT NEEDS TO BE

This is my story. It's what brought me to this place from when I was at my worst. At the height of all the problems that were going on in my life, my biggest realization was that I did not know my childhood. I don't remember anything from when I was about 13 years old and younger. I had therapists and practitioners of all different sorts telling me that I had to remember in order to be able to move past it, or my childhood would stay a reflection of my life. To remember it would enable me to get rid of it and move beyond it.

What I have found out since is that this simply isn't true.

You can resolve your issues without going into the actual memory. You can get rid of the subconscious stress and the trauma without going back through it and bringing it back up in your head. Remember what I said before about talk therapy: the more you talk about it, the more you seal it into that neuroplasticity and the more it sticks in the recesses of your brain.

It turns out that just being able to touch the edge of it and get a feeling for it is enough to clear it, or at least to get a good jump on the process. There is enough information for the chemicals associated with the feeling to be able to clear the issue and start removing the issue from your mind. This is very easy to do.

There are a lot of courses out there that teach all kinds of ways to do this. But at the end of the day, what it boils down to is this: while all these ideas and protocols come with different angles and different teachers, what they're trying to get done is exactly the same. Your body has the function and ability to do exactly what you need.

The difference lies within you and not within the protocol.

I've talked about God a few times, and because of how I was raised, it's my belief that God does exist. I enjoy the stories of the Bible. I think they're fascinating and wonderful, and for me the Bible is alive. It's interesting to see the depth and information that can come out of it when you're just not just reading it from the surface. There is an energy to it, and this is part of what brought me to the beliefs I hold now as an adult. In particular, I have the absolute desire to be able to do what Jesus did because of what we're told. You're going to do greater things. John 14:12-14

In 2016, I was sitting in a conference room in Austin, Texas with an energy psychology group called the Association of Comprehensive Energy Psychology, and a gentleman named Dr. Bill Bengston got up on stage. He said: "You're asking the wrong question." He was speaking about healing with your hands and told us that the question wasn't "Can we heal?" but rather "Why aren't we doing it when we already know we can?"

This man had spent over 20 years carrying out research in scientific laboratories. He would heal cancer-inflicted mice with his hands, which he simply placed around the cage. He says he just sat there for an hour a day. He didn't focus on healing them. He didn't work to heal them and didn't even believe in God. He couldn't feel any energy. But, the mice did change. Over a period of about five days, they all started to heal.

Even more interesting than this was the course I took on Psych-K. The teacher was very engaging. She was very much on the spiritual side of things, although it wasn't the spiritual, or the energy behind the topic, or where that energy came from that I was interested in. It was the protocol itself, and I was curious about whether it was easier to do. I was fascinated with how fast I understood it and already seemed to know it. The basic protocol itself was very simple and came very easily to me. What got my attention was on the second set of lectures during the second weekend, as the protocols were getting more built up and more complex, the teacher did something called a surprise balance. It surprised the heck out of me. During that surprise balance, she didn't really do anything. It wasn't the whole protocol or series of steps. The surprise was that you don't necessarily need the protocol — just make something up and use whatever is available that the person is drawn to that will help them balance. As I took this in, I realized that I didn't need to do any of this. From Dr. Bengston to this surprise balance, I understood that **the difference lies within you and not within the protocol.**

Here's what I have noticed and have had clients tell me. They use a lot of different methods, strategies and protocols. Sometimes they work, and sometimes they don't.

For instance, using tapping, sometimes you tap and tap over and over again but never get anywhere, and then suddenly out of nowhere, you tap slightly on the edge of your pinky and everything melts away. It happens in EMDR too, when you work and work to resolve something that never happens, but then one time outside of the office, you're using a bilateral stimulation like tapping back and forth between your crossed arms and all of a sudden, the result just happens. I can't really explain any of this except to say that we have made this out to be far harder than it should be.

If Dr. William Bengston can hold his hands around a cage and heal the mice inside, and the PSYCH-K lady can do a balance without the protocol, then I think we really are asking the wrong questions. We CAN heal ourselves. I think the question is, "How do we get more efficient at healing and changing the belief structure that says we can't?" Another good question to ask might be, "How can we make this easier?" Can we strip down all the protocols and the systems so that it doesn't take as long?

Using a whole brain state is the quickest thing I've tried that doesn't require all of the protocol that many systems have built around it. I teach people to listen to their body, feel their body, and learn to use the system that is already within them. To be able to clear the subconscious mind effortlessly and rid yourself of symptoms is potentially a life-saving notion.

A whole brain state, in conjunction with a heightened level of emotions, cuts to the chase and gets results faster than anything else I've ever seen. You keep releasing the stress that can turn into subconscious issues. And life becomes totally different. You can get results faster. Your body learns to feel different.

When you add an elevated emotion coupled with an intention in a whole brain state, the results are dramatic. They happen quickly, and then life starts to fall seamlessly into place.

Mind Rewire teaches you how.

Your body has the ability to renew your mind. It is the way God made the system.

Chapter **Eight**

HOW YOUR BODY WORKS

You already have everything you need within your physiology. There's a philosophy for success that I keep on my wall about keeping your beliefs positive. Mahatma Gandhi said it best:

Your beliefs become your thoughts,

Your thoughts become your words,

Your words become your actions,

Your actions become your habits.

Your habits will become your values

and your values will become your destiny.

What is it that you believe? Bruce Lipton said, "Change your beliefs and change your life." Do you believe that what you think has a big role in how your life plays out? If you do, then you'll make a practice every day to wake up and change the things that you're thinking.

If it hasn't been as easy as that for you and you find yourself stuck, it's because of a subconscious issue. It goes deeper than the conscious mind and you need help – something you can do that will help the issue get unstuck so that you can move beyond it and take back control of your life. It's a practice — something you do daily, because life happens daily.

I get a newsletter from a man named Raymon Grace who does his own brand of healing. He is a very interesting person. He says it like this. You can't expect to take a bath once a day and stay clean. Dirt moves, and you will get dirty again. Energy moves, life will happen you have to do your work daily to stay where you want to stay. And be what you want to be.

Every time an issue comes up, every time something happens, you'll have exactly what you need to move it and keep it from turning in to actions, and habits, and emotions that could potentially destroy your life.

The great thing about this is that it also works the same way in a positive sense. Think about how it works from a positive angle by pulling up the most positive thought you can. For me, this is something I once saw in Costa Rica. I was looking over the edge of a cliff and seeing a huge rainbow shining over a waterfall. It makes my heart sing every time I remember it. When I go back to that thought and really think about it, I pull up that same emotion in my system. I can feel my heart opening and my mind starting to become electric.

Your beliefs become your thoughts. Keep that emotion in focus. Keep the emotion, that feeling big inside your system.

Your thoughts become your words. I'm thinking with positive, elevated emotion, what am I saying? Out loud or quietly to myself?

Your words become your actions. Whatever I talk about, I tend to do. If I talk about the crap of the day or continue in the crap of my past, what will my behavior be?

Your actions become your habits. What do you practice? What do you do day in and day out that promotes health and peace in your life?

Your habits become your values. What do you hold onto that is most dear? What do you value in your life? What thing do you do that produces and adds value?

Your values become your destiny. Are you on your God-given path? Or, are you confused and in a heap on the sidewalk of life? Destiny! What is your destiny?

How does it feel when a positive thought is inside your body — when the positive feeling is coursing through your veins instead of the negative ones? What an amazing and interesting outlook. You have the healing mechanisms all built right into your system.

If you keep the positive influx of chemicals in your body over long periods of time, eventually, your system will start to revert back to what it was intended to be. It starts to act and react the way that it's supposed to instead of being caught in the chemicals that keep you mad, stressed, or ill and in constant fight or flight mode.

If your energy is stuck and you're not moving forward in your life, it's necessary to do something that will clear out your energy systems and move forward. You have to get beyond the analytical mind and let the body feel and flow, allowing the good chemicals in that will work for you instead of against you.

How do you make this work? Back in the day, John Lennon said "all you need is love", in a world without chemicals and without all the stress we live in that would probably be very true. How many times have you hit that higher vibration of love and were able to stay there for a prolonged period of time? My guess is that it doesn't happen often, if it happens at all. I believe that all of us can. However, it takes teaching the body how to feel different than it does now.

Right now, you practice staying in the negative stuff every day, because it's easy to do. It's what you are used to.

You don't have to do anything different, but in order to change and become that new person, it takes a daily effort.

I told you a little bit of my story when I was at my worst. I weighed 300 pounds. I had a number of autoimmune issues and seemed to be struggling on a daily basis just to survive. As I got healthier and healthier and started realizing how a lot of this works, I started playing with the system just to see what I could do. I went back to what the Bible teaches, that we are going to do greater things. What does that mean?

This is one of my greater things!

This is my story (and I'm sticking to it). I was standing over a pile of muffins one day that I had bought from Costco. These little muffins were made from good, organic grains, but I still couldn't eat them because my body reacts poorly to grains. I stood there, just looking at those muffins, knowing what they tasted like and really wanting them, but knowing what would happen to my body if I ate any. Then, I put my hands over the muffins and spoke a few words about blessing the muffins to my body, asking the things in the muffins that would benefit me to absorb into my body and the things that wouldn't benefit to do no harm to move straight back out. It sounded strange and I couldn't help but laugh at myself for it, but there was also a voice in my head that said, "Test it and find out if it works, then." Guess what? I ate one and there were no bad effects. Normally, when I eat something, I can

tell when it was something I shouldn't have eaten very quickly. This time...nothing happened.

When you get clear enough that you can hear the voice
of God, this is one of the most interesting parts of how our
body works. One of the healing mechanisms that we have
built into our system is to be able to talk to God, have a rela-
tionship and get to know him. When we can do that, we can
get information quickly and easily. It's a part of what can
make your whole world change so quickly.

Even when working out- I'm talking to my body. To
the cells. To specific muscles and joints. Opening, releasing, strengthening, I have had all kinds of fast results because of my practice of doing this. I believe it is part of
what helped me lose weight when I was my sickest, when
I was working out and had "no hormones" according to
my doctors.

One of the things I do is teach people how to bless their
bodies and food.

How to talk to yourself. To make work outs more effective.

How to talk to what they're eating, you won't have such
a harmful problem in your system. Of course, the smartest
thing to do is stay away from things that have poison in them
from the GMOs and chemicals that our country regularly

puts into our food. In the next chapter, I'm going to be talking about food and nutrition because it also plays a role in this.

The take away here is that you can have an effect on your body, by how you talk to it and to the food you put in it.

Chapter **Nine**

MIND REWIRE IN A NUTSHELL

Mind Rewire is how the body can work for you to release subconscious stress and other issues that are locked into your brain at the level of the subconscious.

How it works

Think of the issue you are facing.

What seems to be causing the problem?

What do you want instead?

While thinking of what you want, sit in a whole brain state and hold that in your system as long as you can.

A **whole brain state** involves thinking of the thing you want while crossing your legs and noticing how it feels. Go the direction that is the most comfortable. If it feels the same to you, just pick a side. Do the same thing with your wrists. While thinking about the issue, find what feels best. Sit in this pattern while you are releasing the issue. Sit in this pattern while you are thinking of the thing you want.

Pull up a big emotion, something that really makes you feel good, and sit feeling this with the thing you want in your mind. Stay in the whole brain state. Within a few minutes, you will feel a shift in your system. This is an indication that you are changing a pattern.

There are some more subtleties to Mind Rewire that come into play when I am working with people that are not listed here. But this is the general idea. It works with life stress, subconscious stress, and can change your perceptions of something in minutes. It will give you a more open approach to perceiving life.

Sometimes, people will have a hard time accessing a feeling that makes them feel good. That is one of the things I tend to be really good at helping people find and circulate through their systems.

Seems too easy, doesn't it? Don't struggle through it! Let me show you how.

Get on that strategy call.

https://mindreiwre.com

After a few sessions, you will begin to know the difference.

It is not something that is easily shown in a book. There is a feel for it. Please don't get on a call with me just to tell me that I didn't tell you exactly how to do this in the book.

You are right I didn't.

Chapter Ten

WHAT ROLE DOES NUTRITION PLAY?

How does my diet play a role in my thinking? And what am I thinking that plays a role in my diet?

I am 60 years old, and I have always struggled with food. It has RULED my life. It ruled it so much that I developed an unconscious fear around it, resulting in many other self-sabotaging emotions and actions. This food fear caused me to consciously make any distracting behaviors I could to tone down the monster that lived inside, because I kept ignoring him! I could never relax around food and enjoy it. It was like a heavy weight on my shoulders.

After my Mind Rewire therapy from Christy Mattoon, I had an amazing transformation. This transformation was tested only 5 hours after my session. My experience as I went to a restaurant with several girlfriends was that I noticed that I no longer agonized over the menu and could sit and enjoy appetizer portions instead of large quantities like I was used to. The most amazing feeling was feeling so relaxed during the dinner and even paying attention to my satiety instead of just stuffing myself till my plate was empty. I even left food in the plate as it did not suit my palate at the time and I was full! When dessert time came... "no" was easy to say with no guilt!! Amazing! I left that restaurant feeling so high... I was ecstatic!

I am grateful for this new Mind Rewire that has helped me to enjoy my life more and not let those old habits run the show! Thanks Christy!

With much gratitude,

Sue

For years, I have heard stories like these and gotten questions about all kinds of diets. What works, and what doesn't? Is this the right diet for me? Am I doing this right? Can I eat this? Can I have that? What if I'm autoimmune? What if I'm diabetic? Why don't I feel better?

Of all the questions and all the possible answers from people around the globe, there is one thing that's for certain: if you don't know what is harming you and what is helping you, then you don't know. And if you don't know, it will be hit and miss as to whether or not your chosen diet will work.

Let's undercut the whole diet idea. Why do you need a diet? Write this down. What is the issue you are facing that you need to diet for? Whatever you wrote down, sit and think about it for a minute. Why is that thing happening to you?

Let's take my weight issue — the reason I was always on diets. Why was I obese, overweight, fat? (I want you to know I mean nobody any disrespect, but I called it fat. It is what was said to me and what I said to myself.) Why was I fat? I had all sorts of answers.

I was big boned.

I had an eating disorder.

I was on medication that caused weight gain.

I was addicted to sugar.

I lived in an emotional home of internal turmoil.

I used food as a tool to calm myself down.

What do you think the problem was? What was the underlying issue? While some might pick one thing and someone else might say it's everything, I want to take it apart for you so that you can clearly see the actual problem. I expand upon this idea in my book on how I healed my autoimmune disease.

Let's take a closer look at the problems I listed.

I'm big boned. My bone density was never an issue. I had it tested more than once over the years. The volume and weight of my bones play a direct role in the weight of my body, but not my weight issue. Without a weight problem, my bones still have good density and are healthy. Big boned — not the problem!

I had an eating disorder. I struggled silently with bulimia on and off for years. While it was not the cause of my weight issues, it was its own food problem. In hindsight, I know it was another tool for coping. I also used it as a tool to judge and punish myself when I ate the "wrong" things. This was a way for my body to be in charge when my brain didn't know what to do. My body had the control card, it was sending signals to my brain that to stay in one piece I had to eat a lot, until I felt horrible and then purge to feel better. It was the "feel better" piece I was needing. It was the only way I could find relief.

I have another client that had some serious junk from her child hood that she had vivid memories of. She knew where her issues came from, and she had tried and worked at it from every angle possible, with different protocols and therapies. No one and nothing ever helped. She said that "people tell me I must like my misery because I refuse to let it go." This made me almost scared to take her on as a client. It also made me really sad for her. I know that feeling. It is a deep, subconscious tragedy.

Yet in the first session, we got all the way underneath her memory of this issue. We moved the emotional attachment to it and started to seed in the things she wanted her younger self to know instead. When she emerged from that session, all she could say was, "Relief, I feel relief…"

It isn't the first time I have heard someone say that. Relief, when felt deeply and for the first time, is an amazing experience. Relief is what I thought I was getting when I was purging from my gorging… But that was not the kind of relief I needed.

Medication. My medication caused weight gain. Do you know the side effects and contraindications of your medications? I did, and I was so hopeful that they were going to relive all of the issues I was told they would, so I dismissed the warnings. Dang it, if I had only known.

What I ended up with because of the medications was a body that was not only emotionally on burn out, it was also physically drained and deteriorated. I was gaining weight and symptoms and more medications faster than anyone could keep up with. The bottom line is to know and pay attention to what the side effects are. More importantly, actively determine if you want to take on the possible side effects. Be conscious in the decision. It can be so hard when you are in it, because nothing is really conscious.

Sugar addiction. I was a pastry chef for 20 some years. I absolutely had a sugar addiction — my body was saturated with sugar. But, this addiction, was resolvable. I found a few tricks that helped, and some people I work with now can even go cold turkey. It is crazy interesting what the body will do when it is told something and the brain believes it.

But, if this is you, I want you to know there is a different way to come at this. If you could stick to the diet, it would probably work. The reality of most diets is that they just are not realistic or sustainable in real life. They are a struggle because of the mindset involved. When that changes, everything can change.

Also, if you are eating chemicals and poisons, your body will have an issue. If you're fueling and informing your body with chemicals and pollution that it cannot decipher and doesn't know what to do with, what do you think it is going to do? It expresses what it is given. If you're fueling and informing your body properly, with information that is usable, it's going to function correctly.

The chemicals and GMOs are breaking down your system. Once an organ tissue or other area wears out and has an issue, there is more damage to repair than is possible from simply improving your diet. In this case, you'll need to take action to heal tissues that are fighting you. You have to stop everything and clean out your physical and mental systems.

Disclaimer: I'm not telling you to drop all medications. This has to be a conscious and informed effort. Consult a homeopathic specialist to help, get someone supportive on your side, and research natural alternatives.

Let your body calm down and give it room to heal. There's no other way to do it. A pill is not going to solve this, and neither is hoping and praying that you land on the right combination of foods. You have to start asking the right questions now: What will my body tolerate? What will exacerbate my symptoms?

Sometimes, fasting is the quickest way to let your body calm down, because it allows the chemicals and stress to come out of your system so that it can recalibrate and reset.

I have a number one bestselling book on Amazon called *How to Combat Autoimmune Disease and Win*. It explains, in detail, how I healed my body. Full disclosure: I still struggle with a few of the symptoms I've had for years, but for the most part, the symptoms are completely gone and my blood work is normal. If I eat the wrong thing, it sets my immune system back off and my antibodies kick up again. My hair starts falling out at unbelievable rates and my body will swell up in certain places with inflammation. But if I eat as I should, they come back into normal range relatively quickly.

What this tells me is that my system has not had sufficient time to get back to health. I test it periodically and clearly need to wait longer to get it to reset. However, it's important to note that I'm constantly talking to my system, to my body. I'm blessing it. I'm feeling gratitude for what it does for me. I take it into meditation and I work with it, giving my body good chemicals to use as far as the system itself is concerned. I give it the food that I know it can utilize as fuel and the information it needs to function normally.

Again, I think that we've made this harder than it needs to be, with diets telling us to do this or do that, don't do this and don't do that. We're told a lot of different things all the time, but when you truly know what your body can use and you truly know what to expect when you eat certain things, there will be no denying what you don't want in your system and what it will allow.

How did I do it? It took a while to get to a place where I could calm down with food, and where I could recognize that food wasn't just a way to satiate my emotions. I was taking everything out of my system, letting it calm down. My immune system was so blown out that I was in adrenal fatigue and having all kinds of crazy problems as a result. Once I quit eating and let the system calm down, it began to come back into balance and I would start to eat again.

Rice was a big offender, as was corn. Anything with gluten in it was horrifying to my system and it wasn't just in my head — the tissue underneath my skin would grow so inflamed that I could physically feel my body blow up like a water bed. When I stayed away from that kind of food, the inflammation went down and my body was fine. It took a while to figure out that some of my fat was not fat, but inflammation produced by my immune system, because my body was fighting to kill invaders that were not invaders. It was doing its job.

Simply knowing what I could eat and what would cause an issue changed the entire scenario for me.

The "Woo-Woo" Side

However, there's no doubt in my mind that if I talk to the muffins to bless them, I can eat one and still be safe. It's an interesting testament to how powerful your mind actually is, how powerful your hands are, and what your body can do in correlation with your thoughts when you just put your mind to it. If I'm only mindlessly eating and have one of those muffins, my body blows up, but talking to my food changes everything. It's something to keep in mind when you're going through all of this. There is another chapter in this book that details how crazy I am, and how I believe that God designed these wonderful bodies and just how powerful they are.

Now, ask yourself: what exactly are you putting in your system? Are you eating harmful chemicals? Are you drinking water that has poison in it? What about the air you're breathing? What about the things you're using to clean with, both your surroundings and your body? All the chemicals involved in all of these products can throw your body off.

Your body will feel good and function properly when it is fueled with information it understands. The chemicals and hormones your body creates naturally wreak complete havoc with your system when you're not in alignment. You can balance them with food and thought.

If it doesn't feel good in your system, don't eat it. The longer you stay away from sugar, for example, the easier it will become. Your body will lose the addiction and you'll be able to move on, but it takes practice. Pay this effort the time, effort and intention it deserves.

If this is an area you're having issues with and you're not getting noticeable results, I will help you come at it from the subconscious to see what can be taken care of there. That will unlock the issue and start to reset the system so that you can control yourself better. Lack of control, either mental or physical, will mess up your trajectory in life.

If your body has control and holds the cards, I will help you reestablish control and re-teach your body how to think and feel. If you're out of control, your cells are sending out signals and the brain is doing what it is told. Feel bad, eat more, don't eat, feel worse... The body knows how to do this all by itself at this point, and does it on its own. You can learn how to teach your body a different way to do it.

This may be a stretch for some, but think about how genes signal the body. The gene knows what to do because of the environment it is in.

Over time, the same environment creates a habit. On a cellular level, a bad habit looks like disease, pain... You either continue in the issues, or you change them.

The information you take in comes from, many places, including old memories, trauma, and beliefs because, they provide your body with chemical information. The chemical information relates to your emotions and is locked into each cell of your body. If they are trained with bad information, your body will keep getting the signals from the chemicals that were expressed at the time of the original insult. You'll find yourself fighting with the same old issues. Can you teach your body to feel differently?

I've have seen people reverse their diseases such as diabetes, Crohn's disease, fibromyalgia, asthma, and even cancer. They do this by taking control of their mind in order to control their body, as well as their environment. Remember, your food is a major part of your environment. So is your mindset.

This is something that anyone, no matter who they are, can take authority of and with the right help, it can happen faster.

You should always first talk with your doctor if you have something like an autoimmune issue. Take their advice seriously, and learn as much as you can.

For more information and to order my book on how I healed my autoimmune disease, go to

https://www.mindrewire.com/my-books/ to order for Kindle or as a paperback.

For a comprehensive strategy session to see if Mind Rewire can help you, go to **https://meetme.so/mindrewire**

Chapter **Eleven**

HAIRY ARM, ALLERGY OR PHOBIA?

People come to me all the time saying that they have what they think is subconscious stress and want to clear out their subconscious mind, but that because they had a good childhood, they don't know where all this stress is coming from.

I have a series of questions that I get people to answer before we start any sessions, including to list their top 10 limiting beliefs. What are the things they are telling themselves inside their own heads? What do they hear? Go ahead — stop right now and list yours. What are the top things that you believe are true about yourself that limit your life in any way?

The next thing I ask my clients to do is to list their three biggest goals. What do they want to do in their life, and what does this look like? Write it out so you can see it and re-read it. I also ask what patterns, if any, they can see happening that keeps them from reaching their goals. I ask what their big, pivotal life moments were. These can help point us in the right direction as well.

However, even without any of this information, we can start from the standpoint of simple feelings. What do you feel like? What is it you're feeling when you go into the issue or pattern that you see happening around you? If your childhood was great but you're still having issues, it means something happened somewhere along the way.

I heard a story once about a girl who had an intense phobia of body hair. As a child, she was going down a playground slide — a very tall slide that was scary to climb up or slide down, because it had a steep ladder and the slide itself was very steep. Of course, this resulted in a lot of stress as the chemicals that cause fear moved through her system. She may have been having some fun, but these were stress chemicals.

A man was leaning against the bottom of the slide, and she could see his arm when she slid down. It was an image that she had locked onto. Hair had nothing at all to do with the slide, but in the sharpest moment of fear, she locked on to the image of this hairy arm and in her otherwise great childhood created a phobia that she wasn't able to shake out of her system. The phobia kept getting bigger and bigger as time went on, until it became a truth. She had a belief that made absolutely no sense. She was scared of hair.

It's important to remember that wherever you focus your eyes and lock your attention, no matter what it is, that something can become a truth. Whether known and done on purpose or unknown and done very unintentionally. She was a child. She had no idea. But wherever you focus your energy, and place your attention you can instantly turn something into a belief.

What might have happened differently if somebody had stopped that girl right then and addressed the issue? It's something you might not think about as a parent, but it's an interesting question to stop and ponder, because this is the kind of thing that can form crazy issues in the future.

Or, what would have happened if she belonged to a family that had a daily ritual of cleansing the day from your system with intention and purpose?

A former client of mine who is now in school in Hawaii for healing and acupuncture had a crazy coughing problem from the moxa they were burning in the school here in the states. Her coughing fits were out of control. She realized it was an allergy to the moxa. Here is her story, as she relayed it me:

I was that person (note past tense), the one that coughed. For more than 3 months, everywhere, throughout the day, always armed with water, a lozenge and tissue, just in case. I annoyed everyone, I was not sick, I managed, treated and cleared all the usual suspects and yet I coughed. I started school for Traditional Chinese Medicine about 2 weeks into this, my poor classmates and instructors, 4 nights a week they endured my coughing. One night in class I realized that the current trigger was moxa, an herb that is used in treatments, it was irritating and triggering my cough. This was a problem and the cough was getting worse.

I was on the phone with you and began coughing, again. I explained that I knew what the issue was and you said it could be cleared with what you do and that we could do it over the phone. You guided me through the process, it was easy to follow and understand. The allergy and emotional stress associated with it were addressed in one session.

That same night there was significant improvement, it was more of an issue of calming my body down from all the irritation and coughing — the more you cough, the more you cough. It is a week later I am able to sit through 4 hours of class and a treatment in the clinic where I was breathing, smelling, and fully aware of the moxa burning all around me and no coughing!

Me Ke Aloha,

Bobbi

What is the difference between an allergy and a phobia? To my mind, an allergy is the body's reaction to a physical stimulus; a phobia is the minds reaction. It is still an issue, still has an emotional component, and can still be cleared the same way.

Chapter **Twelve**

THE KEYS TO SUCCESS

Everybody has their own ideas about how things work and what the best way is to go about fixing themselves. While there are many different methods, protocols, and ideas, there are also a few keys to success that will undoubtedly help set you in the right direction.

One of them is having something in your hip pocket that you can do easily and quickly at any point you need to. Any time there's a circumstance in which you feel uncomfortable in negative feelings, causing chemicals to begin surging through your body, having a way to relieve you in that instant will be beneficial for the rest of your life.

Another one of the keys to success is to turn it into a practice. You have to start practicing something in order to get anywhere. Look around inside your life and see how that is actively affecting you. Doing it the opposite way would be exactly the same kind of practice, but would result in a positive effect. For example, this could be a continual reminder to say something good about yourself, to bless the situation, or to have gratitude for something — especially something that has not happened yet.

Gratitude in particular carries the energetic signature of completion. Think about being at a birthday party and receiving a gift. Your hands are outstretched and you're all ready for that gift. You open it, look at it, and then look up at the person who gave it to you to say thank you. You're grateful for the thing you just received. To turn this kind of idea into an everyday practice, you can try doing it backwards and being thankful for something before it even gets to you, which brings a whole new meaning to the concept of gratitude. Being grateful in your mind for situations that you're thinking you want before they actually occur carries that energetic signal of completion. What it seems to do is collapse time and shorten the distance to whatever you're trying to obtain. It also changes the chemicals of your body and makes you **FEEL** different.

It's the same idea as the law of attraction. How many people do you know who practice L.O.A, saying they spend time repeating the things that they want? They're trying to attract and manifest those things, but usually they never show up. Some get it right, but it doesn't always work. To my mind, that means something must be wrong in the process. Try being grateful before you even get the thing that you want and see what happens. That could make all the difference. Add an elevated emotion to that intention.

That's what Mind Rewire is all about! Making a difference…

Think of all of the time spent doing what you are doing…

What is the yield from it?

What you currently yielding or seeing in your life is proof of your practice.

Doing nothing, will yield nothing.

Doing something will yield that- make sure it is what you want.

Chapter **Thirteen**

EXPERIENTIAL EVIDENCE

Over the years, I have gained a lot of experiential evidence from working with so many people from different countries and walks of life. Evidence is what weighs the most in my mind. Hearing a person say, "Wow, you just changed my life!" is an amazing thing. So is listening to someone chanting quietly, with tears in their eyes, "Relief, relief... this is relief..."

Just the other day, I received an email from a client who said that over the years, she had tried dozens of self-help techniques and therapies that just didn't work permanently. Many of them seemed to help for a while, but in the long term they only made her more aware of her problems and didn't provide any long-lasting results or solutions. Instead, what she was faced with was a never-ending cycle of ups and downs that she just couldn't seem to break. She was still constantly searching for a way to change her life and turn it in the direction she wanted to go. Mind Rewire was just that thing.

She made more progress and permanent changes in just a few short sessions with me than she had in the last 15 years of work. She no longer saw her reoccurring issues and problems as impossible hurdles, because they had melted away until they no longer existed thanks to the methods and corrections that Mind Rewire had provided. She also wrote that I had been amazing to work with and a much-needed miracle in her life, and that she is recommending me to everyone. She said Mind Rewire had not only saved her both time and money, but had also turned the direction of her life around entirely.

Another client, Nicole, wrote to me that she found Mind Rewire to be the perfect tool to bridge the gap between where she was and where she wanted to be. She had struggled with extremely low self-value and the symptoms of a broken heart for as long as she could remember, and Mind Rewire was the method that finally worked to restore a sense of true value and belonging. She could now see that the new decisions she was making were changing her life for the better, forever.

One client who took my online courses was a 74-year-old woman who thanked me for guiding her and for finally putting together all the work that she did over the years.

A man named Dino from Hawaii says he took a chance, and that it was one of the best decisions he had ever made in his life.

A woman named Rose told me that I was one of the most intelligent, caring, and supportive people that she knew when it came to providing guidance. Thanks to Mind Rewire, she had been able to work through many personal issues related to her past, which helped balance out her emotions and literally rewire the way she responded to certain triggers.

These comments came from people who were having difficulties across the whole spectrum, from mental and emotional problems to the physical. Mind Rewire is set up in such a way that it can deal with any kind of issue, no matter how problematic or personal. It helps people get to the bottom of the issues and clear them out permanently instead of working through, talking about, or leaving them to work it out alone and get through the course by themselves. The journey is amazing, and when the brain is clear and the energy can move freely through you, it turns life into a whole different game.

I have people who come to me and tell me that they want scientific proof. To those people, I would ask them to check out the work of people such as Dr. Joe Dispenza, William Bengston, or Dr. Caroline Leaf. As I've said myself before, I'm not a doctor or a scientist. I don't count myself as even a visionary. I have been called many things — healer, boss, teacher, guru, friend, mommy, sweetie… I have been asked if I am a shaman, if I am physic, if I am clairvoyant, clairaudient, clair- this and that..

My response is always the same: I don't know about any of that. I know Jesus and I love the scripture. When I read it, it comes alive and makes my heart sing. I love the stories and the power behind the laws, promises, and concepts. I love how the truths written that are there I can point at and match what I am saying to you. I love that this works for everyone, and I really love that I get the chance to tell you.

What I am is a doer. The evidence I have is based on what I've seen, what people have testified to me after working with me, and of course what using Mind Rewire has done for my own life. My evidential experience is my biggest testimony to how this all can work. I healed my body and changed my life. From a 300lb pastry chef to a two-time number one bestselling author, the creator of Mind Rewire, and teacher, trainer, and speaker, what I do speaks for itself. I stand in awe and gratitude to my creator- The God that puts a song in my heart.

My clients are likewise healing by doing the same kinds of things, and are doing things in their lives that they wouldn't be doing without rewiring their minds- they would be stuck in the same old patterns. While some clients received changes but are still looking to dig a little deeper in order to get the specific kind of change they're looking for, other clients have reported back saying that Mind Rewire has been a miracle that has changed their lives completely.

Join me on a journey of a lifetime with Mind Rewire and Tools for Subconscious Change. It will blow you away. You'll learn how to be self-sufficient and how to do the process, and together we'll work to clear out the issues, no matter how big, that are causing you to stumble the hardest. See how Mind Rewire can change your life for the better.

Book your free 30-minute 30 minuet strategy session today!

Go here to book. Https://meetme.so/mindrewire

Made in the USA
Columbia, SC
14 March 2019